What a Relief a Broken Heart Would Be

Ingrid H. Turner

WHAT A RELIEF A BROKEN HEART WOULD BE

ISBN: 978-1-7332962-3-6

DEDICATION

For Shay

WHAT A RELIEF A BROKEN HEART WOULD BE

BACK TO LIFE

If I give you sex, will you
fill this heart?

This gape, this red
yawning?

Would you stuff it with
sand, or steel, or

anything to satiate
this retch?

It consumes me, I think I

hate me, and
I think maybe

you could love me
or fuck me
back to life?

BALL OF YARN

Tight.

Like a ball
of yarn.

Wrapped
and re-wrapped

warped?

But tight.

That's how
this feels.

MATURITY

You didn't slap my face.

But you chewed on my heart.

You didn't shove me against the wall

but your face, it screwed so tightly, I knew...

you despised me for a moment.

I did my good girl part -

I didn't yell
I didn't curse.

I didn't scrunch my face in response.

I stood in the hurricane of your rage
and I thought at least

you'd say sorry
you'd reach out

you'd come back to me.

But you're still cold
across the bed.

You're blowing by me
in the hall.

Must I swallow this too?

Must I submit
yet again?

BELONGING

Your growing irritation with me -

a crinkled brow
narrowed eyes
that flat pause -

it stings like a jellyfish.

Shocked.
I was just playing in the ocean.

Now I'm down for the count and questioning
everything.

I want to take my belonging for granted again.

BROKEN LITTLE PIECES

My broken pieces are
always trying to be whole, so

they start looking for totality
in your broken pieces, too.

I think me and you are just
shards of glass and light

looking to be complete, but
instead, we slice up our hearts

on each other's jagged edges,
and cry about each other's

broken little pieces.

CUTE STORY

It would make a cute story,
wouldn't it?

We could tell our kids all about
how we met
one rainy night.

You were a hard traveling man
I was bored, a little lonely.
We could talk about how

nobody approved, but love would
never stop with us.
Wouldn't that make a great story?

We could be living a quiet but
lovely life, tucked away
in a little house.

Nothing fancy, just enough for
me and you and
the kids and the dog.

It would make a great story, and
tonight, that crackle
in your eyes -

the way you look at me like I'm

delicious, your hands
soft on a shot glass that

you probably love more than
you'll ever love me.
But the fantasy -

it's fun, right? And we might take it
to bed tonight. I haven't decided.
Is having you enough?

Are you the kind of man who
takes pieces of
girls like me who

fall in love with you, while you
waltz into town
strewing fantasies around that

you're not capable of fulfilling?
Leading us bored girls
on rainy nights

to warm beds out back?
I'm not mad yet.
Not until I say yes

to that leathery face and those
worn out hands. But,
if I do say yes,

WHAT A RELIEF A BROKEN HEART WOULD BE

I'm pretty sure you'll steal me, but
not enough of me, and
too much of me will

be left behind in this boring place,
and just enough of me
will travel with you

leaving most of me here,
stuck, incomplete
wanting a fantasy and

dreading the reality.

DANCING IN THE RAIN

You'd never do this in real life,
but I had a vision of the rain
coming down on a sunny day
and you grabbed me
held me
twirled me
danced with me, you
laughed with me!

I know it's not real.
And I'm not crazy, but -

maybe it's a parallel life to ours?
Maybe a vision of souls
dancing through a storm, and
still laughing because souls -
they don't take it so seriously.
They see the sun, too, and
they know that laughter
belongs in the rain, and

a hard life has joy, too.

DID YOU FALL IN LOVE LAST NIGHT?

Did you
fall in love last night?

With someone else, I mean?

You had such a nice time out with friends
and today you're

spacey, dreamy, kind of
wistful, not at all needy of me.

You look like you're in love.
New love.

Not the kind you've been with me,
that old, settled kind of love.

You're not answering me right away, you're
distracted, hazy, you're not

present with me, not at all.

I ask you, like I'm kidding,
if you've got a crush. Because

you're acting like a girl who
feels tingles up and down her body

and fire in her vagina when she
thinks about a boy.

11

WHAT A RELIEF A BROKEN HEART WOULD BE

You laugh
and I laugh,

like, what a ridiculous thing.

But I was that girl
with you, so

I know what it looks like.

I'm not sure if I want you to tell me, so
maybe we'll leave it for today.

Maybe you'll enjoy your fantasy
and I'll get some things done.

The floors need swept.
Counters need wiped.

And I only clean when I'm upset.

DIVORCE PAPERS

My divorce papers are jamming up the damn printer.

And that's poetic, all things considered.

My friend reminds me three times about the food
upstairs while we're wrestling with it.

I'm focused on re-ordering pages that spilled onto the
floor before we noticed the tray wasn't out -

he's wrenching on the drawer, trying to unstick a
crumpled half page,

there's ink dripping off his fingers -
and he's still talking about food.

"Mmhmm", I respond.
I'm not annoyed.

I just have no idea what form this page goes to.

And I've already eaten, but I forgot to tell him.

So, he tells me about the food again -

That's when it clicks
and I want to cry.

Hey friend, he's saying between the food,

I'm so sorry you're going through this

13

And I love you.

Please eat.

DON'T TAKE YOUR HANDS OFF OF ME

It's funny how
a life

molds us, takes

this soft
white

clay that is

our curious
nature

and hammers
us out.

Sometimes we
bend, and

sometimes
we break.

There's no
telling

what kind
of shape

a life will

WHAT A RELIEF A BROKEN HEART WOULD BE

leave us

in the end.

Just today the
rolling pin

of you, it
flays me

open, bleeding.

It hurts
my love, and

I need you.
So, please,

don't take
your hands

off of me.

YOUR FACE ACROSS MY SCREEN

Every time your face
flashes across my screen, I

pop a little inside. You're
so beautiful, but not in the

traditional sense, I mean
yes, you're handsome and

I like your face, but it's
your energy or maybe just

my fantasy. I have this moment
every time you post something

reflective, with depth, I just
have a moment where our

whole lives span before my eyes -
we're sitting together at night and

drinking red wine and
reading poetry and

laughing, because life is
sweet since we found this in

a huge world, thanks to...
I don't even remember how?

It's usually just that flash and I

WHAT A RELIEF A BROKEN HEART WOULD BE

flick my screen and our life is

gone, relegated to the
chambers of my imagination, but

I have to admit - sometimes the taste
of red wine and what I

imagine is the dark and rich
complexion of your voice, it

lingers - it wafts through my
duties, my kids, my husband, this

job...and sometimes it stays, it
stays for days and days.

FANTASY

At first, the world in my head,
this whole galaxy of you and me -

It was delightful and it made me feel

warm -
drugged, like a heart shaped opiate.

But now this thing has become a monster, and
I'm entirely dependent on a fantasy, and that just

makes you, the real one in front of me,
gray, opaque –

dirty and needing a wash.

FIREFLIES

"What do you love most?"
He asked her, like
the question proved something.

"Fireflies," she said.

"You mean lightning bugs?"
He smirked, like
maybe he was playful.

"Whatever," she said, and
walked away.

HEARTBREAK

Heartbreak. What a relief
a broken heart would be.

Instead, my heart is bending,
kept pliable by hope.

You're sitting so close to me
on the narrow edge of

misunderstood, separated only by
one perspective shift.

But my body isn't long enough
to bridge a gap of things

misspoke, too often, rushed
left unsaid, hanging.

This bed is leagues of desert
dried up passion, rotten fruit.

"I would give anything" - so says
that saboteur, a hopeful heart.

I have learned nothing
but this: my beggar's heart is

grossly
    compulsively
        predictable.

I AM EMPTY OF YOU

I am empty of you
like a dried out
wash

parched

at the dusty end
of a bone dry
summer.

I DON'T WANT A DIVORCE, BUT

I don't want a divorce.
but I don't see another way
without asking you to
change, and
I can't imagine you're willing to do that.
Why would you?
Not for me.
It takes years
they say,
and honestly,
I don't know if I can wait.
I like to think I would
if you were really doing it.
The work, I mean.
Wait, I mean.
But you're so good at showmanship
I don't trust myself any more so
how will I know if it's real or just
smoke and mirrors.
God damn it, I wish you were
who you said you were
when I married you
when I stood at the altar
and put that ring
and all of me
on your finger.
I've never committed so fully
to anything.
How can I pull back
from something like that?
I don't want a divorce
but I don't want to be with a man like you.

I KNOW IT'S JUST A MOMENT

I know it's just a
moment between us, but

I don't trust this
tension, that distant

look on your face, I
think it might

stretch out forever
to the end of us.

WHEN YOU COULDN'T GET ENOUGH

I miss the days when you couldn't get
      enough of me.

When your hands crawled over my body in
      a frenzy.

When your lips brushed over my skin,
      shuddering

and you bit down a little with delight,
      titillating.

I miss how you looked at me
      blazing.

How you licked your mouth, almost
      gasping.

The way every piece of you was in
      reverence of me.

I'm looking at you now – listless,
      bored, agamous.

They say the marriage bed is cold but I'm
      broiling, on fire

desperate to dispel my want, my need, to
      evaporate me

find me some relief, laying here missing

25

our sex.

Tonight I miss your desire for me, I'm
       aching

but I'll lay quiet I guess, and just converse
       with my regrets.

I'M NOT BUILT FOR YOUR LOVE

I'm feeling
stuffed.

Crammed into
a box the size of

your arms.

This is love
I'm told -

to feel this
tight,

immobile.

"I love you"
you say.

"I love you, too"
I reply, but I'm

confused why

am I so
squirrely, so

desperate to
escape this

warm place, this

embrace?

I cannot breathe
with your arms

around me
like this.

I'm not built
for your love, and

I'm so sorry, baby.

NOTHING AT ALL

Your words are saturated
in emotional poverty

"Let
        Me
                Go!"

You look at me with
        dough in your eyes
                and say to me

                        "but I'm not doing anything at all!"

And how can I counter that?

HOW ANGRY I AM AT YOU

I'm thinking about how angry I am at you -

drinking my coffee
watching the light
creep over the trees.

It's a beautiful scene but
most of me is traveling along
this vein of resentment instead of
tiptoeing along sun beams.

I'm so angry at you, and yet here I am:

sipping coffee.
You're asleep.

Blissful, unaware -
always unaware, it seems.

I'm stuck in this tug of war between
memory and hope.

Like one day you'll
snap back to your old self

and all my rage will melt.

That vein inside me, the one that
cuts through my heart, breaking it

30

WHAT A RELIEF A BROKEN HEART WOULD BE

piecemeal.

It'll dissolve into love again, and
I'll regain that feeling of

being beautiful, and
wanted, and
adored, and

devoured
by you.

I miss you so much, and that -
that's what keeps me here.

Watching the sun come up
on another day.

Hopeful and
regretful and
desperate-full.

Damn you.

Maybe tomorrow I'll
follow the vein and leave.

Maybe.

GLITTER

I'm wearing a little
glitter today and

that feels nice.

I keep having to
find ways to

feel beautiful. I mean

even though you're
right there, you're

miles away, and

I'm suffering.
I'm disappearing without

the sun of your smile,
the wind of your words.

There's still time, you

can bring me back to life
if you'd only look this way.

YOU SHOULD HOLD BACK

'Let's see where this goes,' you say.
'Maybe I'll love you in a month?'

It's smart to hold back, friend.

I don't know who I'll be in a month
let alone next week,

and who cares to fall in love like that
over and over again?

I've got this habit of soaring with stars.
And nebulas change you, man.

I can't do slow and steady, it's got to be
the moon or the molten core

the surface will never do.

You're right to hold back.

You don't know
who that me
might be

tomorrow
or ever?

"I'll see ya," you say.
I doubt it.

But I don't tell you that today.

MISSING SEX

It's late.

Or early.

It's very late
and very early

and I'm tossing
and turning

the heat is steaming but
that's not what's keeping me up.

I'm tossing this way and
seeing your face

I'm tossing that way and
seeing your back

broiling muscles and now
my hands are involuntarily

scraping the air like
you're on top of me again.

But they whip back and I'm just
scratching my face again

wanting you so bad
in this heat, wanting

your heat.

I can't sleep.

It's very late and
it's very early.

Moonlight won't give it up to
day just yet but oh,

I am buzzing from
tip to groin

remembering the curve of your
the gasp of your
the heat of your...

Oh, God, it is hot!
And I'm just craving

more heat -
your heat.

I can't sleep.

It's very late and
and very early

and I'm asking myself this:

will I ever sleep again?
my body is vibrating like

WHAT A RELIEF A BROKEN HEART WOULD BE

you're riding my orgasm
up and down my insides.

Will I ever sleep again
if I can't have you tonight?

NEEDING YOU

I'm getting better -
though I'm not really thinking of you less.

It's more a static than a blaring horn.
And I think that's improvement.

You're slowly fading into the background.
I'm functioning better during the day.

There's still a clamp on my mind
and a hole in my heart -

and I wouldn't say the clamp is looser,
and I wouldn't say the hole is smaller -

but somehow, I'm growing around you
and I guess I don't need you anymore

even though I still want you more.

I can live with that -
the wanting of you.

It's the needing of you that kills me.

OUR FIGHT

A lump in my throat

Nausea.

It's still cool this early.
A slammed door drops like thunder.

Half of me wants to scream.
The other half: stunned into silence.

It's been one of those fights
where I don't know if I'll ever see you again.

PARIS

I've already forgiven you but I haven't told you yet.

Not sure what that means for us.

Part of me has already forgotten how bad it hurts

and the parts that remember seems to be

dissolving into daydreams with you...

fantasies fueled by a past so perfect it's Paris all over
again.

We never went to Paris, but I heard about it in someone
else's poem

and I like it for us.

It's distant and romantic and I'm hoping it'll keep me
from telling you

that all is forgiven and I love you again, because

we're not in Paris, darling, and the sensible me sees

it's too long a flight, and
we'd never survive it.

SELF DESTRUCT

I always thought
you were the one

I could blame

for all my rage and
all my pain, but

today, you reached

out tenderly, and
I recoiled

even as I am

desperate for your
touch, your affection,

your need of me.

And that's when I
realized I just

use you to self destruct.

SHAKESPEARE

Hey,

I'm sat with my fingers
hovering over the keyboard,

just vibrating, pulsing with
pent up heat, but somehow...

silent.

I don't have anything to say to you.

It's all for me.

I've been sitting here for weeks,
twisting, trying to find torque, or rather -

the words I can say that will finally stop me gasping -
and give me some fucking peace.

But there are no words.
There is no peace.

You are what you are - a creature so daringly beautiful -

made perfectly in the image of my missing parts.

We fit like a possessed puzzle -

I'm ripping off my scabs so I can expose myself to you.

All the work I've done to get better

WHAT A RELIEF A BROKEN HEART WOULD BE

to heal from my childhood -

it doesn't mean damn thing.

Because I want you.
Just consume me already.

This has nothing to do with the quality of man you are.

You're a surrogate for my childhood cravings,
the kind even my parents couldn't feed.

The creature I'm gobbling isn't real.
it's just shadows on the cave wall.

I could blame you for my fire,
for my burn,
for my desire

to be swallowed by you.

But it would be a lie.

Whether you were careless with my feelings
or oafish in your commitment to me -

(and you were)

I demanded things of you
and dressed you in a sick sort of drag.

And you resisted.
Rightfully so.

WHAT A RELIEF A BROKEN HEART WOULD BE

Our time together was always going to end in tragedy
because that's the way our pieces fit together.

I want to blame you.

But in the end, why?

It's all just Shakespeare.

SPACE

There's a gaping space between us
since last night.

I know I didn't mean to hurt you.
But do you?

This crevasse, we keep
trying to bridge it

with pleasantries

smiles
short hugs,

kisses, even.

So far, I just feel
the pressure of space

but I suppose we'll make it back.

That's what lovers do, right?

We always come back.

Tell me we'll come back!

SPIRAL FRACTURE

The love I thought would last forever
is twisting -

a spiral fracture.

The break is happening slowly and
it's agony.

I'm feeling each sliver of bone
snap and ping.

It's truly a death by
a thousand very tiny cuts, but

that's a lot of blood.

You'd think we could stop this,
that we could stop

twisting, that our cries of
pain would endear us to

stop. To halt.

To forgive
and let go.

But that's not what's happening.

WHAT A RELIEF A BROKEN HEART WOULD BE

We are becoming more
deformed as we

bend ourselves in
unnatural ways that

break us into
bits that turn into

a mess, a violent pile of
jutting bones.

Hideous, yes, but,
can you turn away now?

TELL ME EVERYTHING IS OKAY

Tell me you love me and
everything is okay.

I know it's not because
you pull away
your eyes don't stay
your thoughts stray

but don't tell me about it.

Tell me you love me and
everything is okay.

I know it's not, but
can you lie today?
Pretend with me because
I'm not ready

I'm just not ready for this.

Tell me you love me and
everything is okay.

Then I'll smile and
pretend I believe you and
we can carry on like this

just for today.

THE FLOWERS YOU BOUGHT ME ARE PINK

The flowers you bought me are pink.

Pastel.
Friendly.

Of course, I want to exclaim delight

But the fact of the matter is
the flowers you bought me are pink.

Pastel.
Friendly.

What drew you to these in the store?

Absent-minded thoughtfulness?

Pink says:

Chatty.
Surface.

Let's keep it light.

Our whole life is pink.

Don't you see me craving red?

WHAT A RELIEF A BROKEN HEART WOULD BE

Deep.
Carnal.

Can't you see through my pretty smile
to my husky needs?

Do you not see my jaw clenching?

Do you not see my hands
scraping along my thighs?

Why are you set on pink?

Pastel.
Friendly.

When I'm dripping with red over here.

THE LILIES ARE DYING

The lilies are dying.

The petals are becoming translucent
like they are collecting dust from the inside
dimming, wide-eyed white

turning to
dreary, dreamy, dewy.

I hope this isn't about us.

I hope our light
isn't turning dingy,
becoming rote with routine

redundant and
bound, bored, blue.

The lilies are dying, and

dear - I really think
we should replace the lilies.

IT'S OKAY, THE RAVEN TOLD ME

"What do you love best about me?"

I flashed you my biggest smile
when asked that silly question.

You mumbled
and shrugged me off.

No time for such games.

I was disappointed because
I know it's silly but

I love hearing you
loving me, because

I'm always telling you
why I love you.

You don't want to
play the game today,

and that's okay, because
the raven answered me.

The one perched on the
picnic table we just drove by.

The raven told me everything

51

all the nameless

and wordless things,
the raven said them all

to me, in all of me

while you lost interest,
and the raven kept rolling

and telling me every
wonderful thing about me.

So, I don't need it from you.
Don't bother to tell me

Through your irritation
and your sighs.

I don't need anything from you
because the raven,

the raven told me everything.

WE LOST EACH OTHER

We lost each other in
the dribble of days.

We lost each other in
distractions, petty things

silly things we forgot
a day or two later.

We lost each other in
ruts and routines

gliding past one another
forgetting to touch

forgetting that love
doesn't feel like this.

We lost each other when
we forgot that life can

eat passion alive with its
fat, meandering lazy.

We lost each other when
we surrendered to

comfortable, static, this
blaring status quo.

WRUNG OUT

Wretched.
Wrung out.
Strung out.

I don't understand how

one human
I went my whole life
without

can spin me

twist me
fling me
in a million

directions

the moment
I let him
near me.

YOU TOLD ME I LAUGH IN MY SLEEP

You told me I laugh in my
sleep. Like, a lot.

I'm glad you told me, darling.

I'm glad my dreams carry me to
frolicking fancies, while my

waking life is heavy right now.

I feel relief that I seem to
break away when I

sink below these weighty days.

I'm glad you told me how I
laugh when I sleep.

I'm relieved to be made aware that

my mind is still a happy place, even
when I'm exhausted, dredging

up this gravel and this granite, it's

so fucking heavy, my love,
and it's all damn day.

CRAZY UP THERE

You're crazy up there
spinning notes and penning poesy

in all your sultry madness
painting with your messy innards.

It's required of all the greats
who dictate from Celeste.

I got your love note
doubled me over in a dream.

And I'm happily drowning
in your oceanic depths.

We've mingled spirits for a spell.
Deep. Palpable. Carnal.

'Dear God, give me more'
I've moaned and moaned.

I love you.
I do. I do.

But there's an impasse ahead
questions to face.

I've got this offer for you
or a request, if you prefer:

Will you run naked with the wolves

by my side through snow and sleet?

I'm bounding toward the edge
for a swan dive off the bluff.

Will you hold my hand
and make it a lovers' leap?

My sword is drawn
I've become the beast.

Will you charge the gates
and match my scream?

Dear love, my soul
will you? Will you?

I will be running
and leaping
and baring my teeth

I'll be banging on gates
and wrestling the deep.

I'll do it on my own if I must
shaking under destiny's stars.

But I would accept a little refuge
in your warm, kindred heart.

WHAT A RELIEF A BROKEN HEART WOULD BE

ABOUT THE AUTHOR

Ingrid H. Turner is a writer and poet exploring spirituality and the complexity of the human experience. Her writing is rooted in lived experience and emotional truth, blending tenderness with unflinching honesty.

She is the author of multiple poetry collections and spiritual works, and she writes weekly personal essays on Substack.

You can find her writing at:
ingridhturner.substack.com

Find all of her books here:
books.by/ingridhturner

www.ingramcontent.com/pod-product-compliance
Lightning Source LLC
LaVergne TN
LVHW041236080426
835508LV00011B/1241